THE
RIVER
OF
LIFE

THE
RIVER
OF
LIFE

FRANCIS
FRANGIPANE

Whitaker House

Unless otherwise indicated, all Scripture quotations are taken from the *New American Standard Bible*, © 1960, 1962, 1968, 1971, 1973, 1975, 1977 by The Lockman Foundation. Used by permission.

Scripture quotations marked (NIV) are from the Holy Bible, *New International Version*, © 1973, 1978, 1984 by the International Bible Society. Used by permission.

Scripture quotations marked (KJV) are taken from the *King James Version* of the Bible.

Scripture quotations marked (PHILLIPS) are from *The New Testament in Modern English*, © 1958, 1959, 1960, 1972 by J. B. Phillips, and © 1947, 1952, 1955, 1957, by The Macmillan Company.

THE RIVER OF LIFE

Francis Frangipane
River of Life Ministries
P.O. Box 10102
Cedar Rapids, IA 52410

ISBN: 0-88368-453-5
Printed in the United States of America
Copyright © 1993 by Francis Frangipane

Whitaker House
30 Hunt Valley Circle
New Kensington, PA 15068

3 4 5 6 7 8 9 10 11 / 06 05 04 03 02 01 00 99

Contents

Introduction

Descending from the glorious headwaters of God's throne, the psalmist tells us, *"There is a river whose streams make glad the city of God"* (Psalm 46:4). Ezekiel tells us that this Eternal River flows into this world through the temple of God. Not only does it turn bitter waters into sweet, but *"everything will live where the river goes"* (Ezekiel 47:9).

It was Jesus Himself, however, who directed the course of the River. It would not flow through a temple made of stone, but through the inlet of His disciple's yielded hearts. He said, *"He who believes in Me...'From His innermost being shall flow rivers of living water'"* (John 7:38).

The church I serve is called River of Life Ministries. We are an average-sized church with, generally speaking, average people. Yet, God has given us a vision. It is our conviction that, if we return to the standards Christ set for His first century disciples, this River of Life will flow out from us. If we step into the River's flow and allow it to carry us, we are convinced that our churches and our cities can be healed.

Throughout the world the River of Life is rising. In hundreds of cities Christians are gathering together for prayer and, as they intercede, the Holy Spirit is being released, bringing healing power to our world. Even as you read, the water of life is rising, encouraging us all to enter deeper into the awesome purposes of God at the end of this age.

Francis Frangipane

The
Church

*The River, which brings
healing to the nations,
flows from beneath the altar
of hearts consecrated
to God in prayer.*

1

The Son's Great Prayer

*If you believe in Christ, and believe He is the only begotten of the Father, then be assured, Jesus will have all His prayers answered. A time is coming, and now is, when both heaven and earth shall respond to Jesus' prayer, **"that they may all be one"** (John 17:21).*

11

Jesus, the Same Forever

On the night before He died, the most somber night in Jesus' life, the Lord brought His most lofty request to God. He prayed for oneness in His church. Christ's prayer is both visionary and practical considering that, on that same evening, an argument arose among His disciples as to which of them was the greatest (Luke 22:24). In spite of their immaturity, selfish ambitions, and envy, Jesus harbored no second thoughts or unbelief when He prayed that they may all be one.

Even as the Son of God appealed for them, be assured He is praying for us now. *"Jesus Christ is the same yesterday and today, yes and forever* (Hebrews 13:8). He will never lower His standards (see John 12:48); He will not modify His promises (see Matthew 24:35); and His intercession will remain unfailing until we attain His goal for us in God (Romans 8:34; Hebrews 7:25).

To know Christ is to know His heart toward His church. Once again, look at His relationship with His disciples that Passover night. If an observer compared the instructions of Christ with the responses of His disciples, he would have concluded that there was little communication between them. Jesus presented His vision of a church motivated by His love and humility. In contrast, His disciples dwelt in carnal desires and weaknesses. Consider that while Jesus prayed they would be *"perfected in unity"* (John 17:23), the only unity the disciples knew that night was a common fear and a collective abandonment of Christ. Consider this: Jesus told these soon-to-be leaders of the Jerusalem church that they would be known for their untiring agape love, but that night Christ's three closest friends could not remain awake with Him even one hour while He agonized alone in prayer.

His disciples were deaf to His promises, blind to His sacrifice, and ignorant of His vision; they were without revelation, obedience, or courage. Yet, in spite of themselves, Jesus told these very men, *"He who believes in Me, the works that I do shall he*

*do also; and greater works than these shall
he do"* (John 14:12).

How could they ever attain His works?
Oh, the grace and love of Jesus! They
would do His works because He was about
to *"go to the Father"* (John 14:12), where
He would ever live to make intercession for
them!

There have always existed two realms
in the definition of the church: one is the
place of beginnings, the disciple's world,
cluttered with human fears and worldly
ambitions. The second reality is the place
of destination, the eternal, glorious realm
that Jesus died to give us. The Living Span
bridging both is Christ's cross and intercession. Any time the church awakens to
the promises of God, the way to holiness
and power is already there. Christians
must only agree with the Father's plan.

The shallow, immature level of the
church has never stopped Christ from praying for its perfection. He could no sooner
stop praying than cease being the Son of
God. Jesus is the Redeemer of mankind.
Even in wrath, His motive is redemption!

Christ's Commitment to His Church

Jesus has always known the frailty of His church. He knows that when we commit our lives to Him, it is not a commitment that says, "I will never sin again; I will always be good." Try as we may, if we could keep such a resolution, we would not have needed Christ to save us!

Our salvation is not built upon what we do, but upon Who Jesus becomes to us. Our commitment to Him is an acknowledgment that we have come to the end of ourselves: we *need* a savior. Having thus discovered no righteousness within us, we have entrusted both our condition and our future to Him. We commit ourselves to obey Him, but we frequently fail. We are required to know His Word, but we barely understand it. We pledge ourselves to follow, but how often we find ourselves lost!

Our salvation is an abandonment to His ability to keep that which we have committed unto Him (2 Timothy 1:12). He who thinks otherwise has never come face to face with his need for God. As the Lord's church, we must each discover the sustaining and renewing power of Christ's prayer. Without such knowledge, we will be overwhelmed by the many times we fail.

Peter discovered Christ's unchanging commitment that last night. Though others failed, Peter boasted of his commitment; he would not fail. However, Jesus told His upstart disciple how, that very night, he would deny His Lord three times. Not only did Peter fail, but all Christ's disciples deserted Him that night. What was the Lord's reaction? Did He chasten Peter, express His personal offense, or shame him? No. Although there are times when Christ must rebuke us, Jesus prayed that, though Peter would fail, his faith would continue and he would be a strength to his brothers (Luke 22:32).

Immediately after warning Peter of his impending denial Jesus further comforted His disciples. He encouraged them, *"Let not your heart be troubled; believe in God, believe also in Me"* (John 14:1). While this verse is suitable for calming any troubled heart, Jesus was speaking uniquely and compassionately to His disciples. Incredibly, it was Jesus, about to go to the cross, who comforted the very disciples who were about to deny Him!

We do not truly know Christ until we have failed and find Him still our friend, drawn ever closer to us by our repentance and our need. What is true concerning His devotion to us as individuals is true concerning His commitment to a repentant citywide church as well. Our failings have not disqualified us from God's purposes. If we turn and trust Him again, we will find that the same Lord who requires we obey Him remained our Redeemer and Intercessor when we failed Him.

The Father's Unchanging Purpose

Two things exist that are greater and more enduring than the failings of the church. According to Scripture, these two things are *"the unchangeableness of* [God's] *purpose"* (Hebrews 6:17) and the permanent, priestly intercession of Christ (Hebrews 7:24–25).

Jesus, intimately familiar with the holy intentions of the Father, knows that it is not God's will for the church to be fearful, ambitious, or jealous. Christ can pray with confidence for divine love, unity, and glory to adorn His church, for these are God's will.

Jesus' prayers are always answered because He only prays for what is already in the Father's heart. The confidence of Christ's prayer is based upon His own personal virtue, not that of the church. Through His sacrifice, *"He is able to save forever those who draw near to God through Him"* (Hebrews 7:25). This same verse in the King James Version reads: *"he is able also to save them to the uttermost..."* Thus, the price has been paid, not only to bring us to heaven when we die, but to bring the life of heaven here where we live.

It seems that the Lord's disciples frequently carried the burden of wrong attitudes and aberrant concepts. Yet, in spite of their immaturity, Jesus unhesitantly prayed for the most holy of possibilities: that they would become the human abode for the Trinity of God—a promise that was almost blasphemous to an Old Testament mind (John 14:16–17, 23)!

When we unite with Christ in His purpose and His prayer, eternal life is released for our need on earth. His prayer is the water that flows from the throne of God; He is the River of Life that sustains and directs every move of God. No soul is saved that He has not first died for; no relationship is healed but what comes forth originally from His intervention.

What happens when we agree with Christ in prayer? As we persevere, a circuit of life is completed between heaven and earth. Christ's prayer carries us into the provision of God; our prayer, united with His, brings God's provision back to the need. The revivals and harvests we see emerging around the world, the collapse of communism, and the exodus of Jews back to Israel were all birthed as individuals agreed with the intercession of Christ and the plan of God.

Do we truly believe what God has provided for us in holiness, power, and glory? If so, let us persevere with Christ in confidence, knowing that all the Father has given will be brought to earth through prayer.

2

A PROPHECY:
The Prayer of Christ Answered

A *time is coming, and now is, when the Father shall answer the prayer of His Son: **"that they may all be one"** (John 17:21). Imperceptibly at first, but increasingly more as the return of Christ nears, the Father will work in the hearts of many Christians. In answer to the prayer of His Son, true followers of the Lord Jesus will lay aside their differences and return to Christ as their first love.*

21

Without any official change of doctrine, denominational church leaders will begin to downplay their differences and, in sincerity and truth, refocus their love upon Jesus. From many biblical perspectives the church shall return to the simplicity and purity of devotion to Christ.

As the Father answers the prayer of His Son, the living church will discover blessings and power it formerly assumed were for the age to come. With each step toward Christ, joy and righteousness will multiply. The miraculous will become ordinary in the extraordinary presence of Christ.

The unity of the church will not be contrived or manipulated. It will be a harmony of divine purposes; it will feel natural and without pressure to conform. Indeed, the strengths of all will be multiplied as churches from different backgrounds recognize God's anointing and calling upon others. Instead of rivalry and competition, churches will be enriched and equipped by one another.

The wholeness the church attains shall come before Christ returns; its unity will be an outgrowth of their oneness with Jesus. Their oneness shall not be born of compromise, but of love. They will not be united merely in doctrines, but in the name, the word, and the glory of Jesus their Lord (John 17:11, 20–22). Indeed, having been perfected into a unit, they shall know the mystery of the eternal love enjoyed by the Godhead and promised by Jesus (John 17:23). They shall walk in the holy fulfillment of Christ's prayer: **"that they may all be one; even as Thou, Father, art in Me, and I in Thee, that they also may be in Us"** *(John 17:21).*

Although the apostate church will challenge it, and the accuser's slander and misinformation shall oppose it, Christ's glory shall be seen in His church. The outcome will be that vast multitudes in **"the world [will] believe"** *(John 17:21). On an unequaled scale, revival shall come to the earth.*

In spite of terrible darkness covering the earth, the glorious fire of God's presence, released through His purified church, shall preserve entire cities and regions.

23

Working together, believers shall gather the Lord's harvest from many nations.

Be assured, Jesus has prayed, and oneness in the church shall occur. For the Father always answers the prayers of His Son.

3

The Surrender of the Vision Keeper

*T*he time is at hand when the Lord Jesus shall confront our tendencies to control Him. Not only will we know doctrinally that Christ is Lord, but we will also serve Him as Lord.

Churches in Transition

If you find yourself more drawn toward prayer than promotion, more toward

25

humility than hype, you are being prepared by the Lord for the next move of God. What He is working in you is typical of what God is establishing in thousands of other believers.

However, before the Father ultimately reveals Christ as Lord over the earth, He will first reveal Him as Lord over the church. While we rejoice, we must take heed because, until we are standing face-to-face in glory with Jesus Himself, we are going to be in transition. To each of us, Christ's call remains, *"Follow Me!"* (Matthew 9:9). If we obey Him, He will take us into the fullness of His presence.

Still, transitions can be frightening. The uncertainty of being somewhere between spiritual plateaus can hold us hostage to yesterday's blessings. Let us recall with godly fear that the bronze serpent, which brought healing to Israel in the wilderness (Numbers 21:9), had become an idol that had to be destroyed by Hezekiah's day (2 Kings 18:4). Our hearts must bow to God alone, for even spiritual gifts, when isolated from the Giver, can become idolatrous.

Therefore, to successfully navigate this season of change, God is requiring of us a fresh surrender to Christ's Lordship. All our preconceived ideas must be submitted to God. For if we are instinctively following our own human expectations, we disable ourselves from finding heaven's best for us.

Christ in Us

To better understand the changes God is initiating in the church, we are going to study the life of Mary, Jesus' mother. More blessed than any other woman, Mary alone was overshadowed by the Most High and granted the wondrous privilege of giving birth to Christ.

While the Lord's purpose with Mary was unparalleled, in two significant ways His promise to us is similar. First, while Mary received Christ into her physical body, we have received Jesus into our spirits. Second, as she gave birth to Jesus, so our quest is to see Christ released from the womb of faith, so that He is no longer contained within us as an internal promise, but revealed through us as Lord to the external world.

Even now, abiding within our spirits, deeper and more profound than our church doctrines, is the actual Spirit of Christ. The consequence of this union of Christ's Spirit with our spirits expands the original seven creation days into an "eighth day," a new beginning in God's eternal plan. In this second genesis, Jesus Christ is the first-born of a new race of men. As Jesus was both God and man, so the church is actually Christ and truly mankind. There is not a different Christ in us than He who dwells in heaven. He is Christ wrapped in glory in heaven; He is Christ wrapped in human flesh on earth.

Our salvation is nothing less than the Perfect One dwelling in the imperfect ones; the Almighty abiding in the feeble; the All-Sufficient God tabernacling among insufficient people. This is the mystery and glory of our salvation: Christ in His completeness has extended Himself into us!

Crucial to the success of His mission is our receiving these truths with faith. We must fight the temptation to allow these truths to become merely our theology. To fulfill our destinies, they must become our reality. It is here, in this carrying of the actual presence of Christ within us, that we share with Mary the awe of God's purpose with us.

Jesus in Subjection

While Joseph was a good man, it was Mary who nurtured Jesus and continued to raise Him after Joseph had died. In fact, we will see that Mary became the matriarch of the family. Uniquely, under her spiritual influence, Jesus matured. It was natural that, over time, Mary would consider herself the "Keeper of the Vision and Guardian of Him Who Is to Come." In truth, she was.

"He continued in subjection to them" (Luke 2:51). This is an astonishing thought: Jesus, Lord of heaven, was in subjection to a lowly carpenter and his wife. Yet if we think about it, is it not equally astonishing that the rule of Christ

in His church is, at least in part, subjected to our initiatives? He submits Himself to our schedules and service times. Do we not act as the senior editors of His truth? Candidly, is it a voice from heaven or earth that determines how long we worship Him Sunday morning?

Yet, if the Lord so decided, in an instant He could reveal His majesty and exact trembling surrender from all mankind. However, He restrains Himself, choosing not to intimidate, but to inspire our obedience. He has chosen to hide His glory not from us, but in us. And then, in order to perfect our characters, He subjects Himself to our initiatives of hunger and faith.

Yet, the fact that Jesus will accommodate and submit Himself to the conditions we offer Him does not imply that He has approved of our limitations upon Him. The standard of the church is not the church; it is Christ. And this is our present dilemma: just as Jesus subjected Himself to Mary and Joseph and they became the "Vision Keepers" for a time, so we have assumed that Christ's present "subjection" to us is sanctioned by God. It is not. If we will truly see Jesus in His Lordship, revealed in His power, He must first deliver us from our efforts to control Him.

A Time to Let Go

It is significant that Mary still exercised matriarchal supervision over Jesus even after He was a mature man. At the wedding feast in Cana, we find Jesus, His disciples, and Mary. *"They have no wine"* (John 2:3), she told Jesus. The Lord answered, *"Woman, what do I have to do with you? My hour has not yet come"* (v. 4). In spite of what Jesus just said, Mary told the servants, *"Whatever He says to you, do it"* (v. 5). While I am amazed at the fact that the Father worked through Mary's orchestration of this miracle, the fact is that Jesus did not come to do the will of His mother, but rather His Father's will. It was time for Jesus, Mary's son, to begin His ministry as Jesus, God's Son.

A significant and necessary reversal of authority was needed in the relationship

Mary had with Christ, a change that she had not anticipated. In her mind, her sense of influence was simply a continuation of her God-given responsibility as the vision keeper.

"After this He went down to Capernaum, He and His mother, and His brothers, and His disciples; and there they stayed a few days" (John 2:12). The verse reads, *"He and His mother"* went to Capernaum. Do you see? Mary, the "Keeper of the Vision," had taken what she thought was a legitimate position, an earned place of influence with Christ.

In Mary's defense, she clearly had been with Jesus the longest. She had paid the highest price. It was Mary who heard the word and believed it. She had served the purposes of God well. Among those human influences in Jesus' life, she was the most blessed and consistent personality. Perhaps she had every right to assume that, in the outworking of Christ's ministry, He would work the miracles and she would remain the guiding influence. Her continued "mothering" was not evil, but natural.

However, God had determined it was time for Jesus to be unfettered from all human influences of control. Jesus would now only do the things that He saw His Father do. And this, I believe, is where God is jealously directing us: we are being emptied of our agendas, false expectations, and non-biblical traditions so that Christ alone will be Lord over us.

A Sword Will Pierce Your Heart

No matter how true a vision from God may be, it will never be fulfilled as we have imagined. All our expectations are incomplete. In fact, our very ideas can become the most subtle obstacles standing between us and our appointed future. Thus, we must keep our minds soft and submitted to God, for His plans will be full of many surprises. When God fulfills His word, it is always *"exceeding abundantly beyond all that we ask or think"* (Ephesians 3:20).

Interestingly, to help Mary in her spiritual transition, we find Jesus resisting her. Before the Lord can bring any of us into a new phase of His will, He must dismantle a certain sense of attainment that, at times, accompanies our relationship to His will. It is a fact that many church movements, both in and out of denominations, began very simply. Hungry souls longed for, and found, more of God. As their numbers grew, "success" replaced hunger, and people became more satisfied with God's blessings than with His presence. For the Holy Spirit to bring us into further glory successfully, He must first dismantle our satisfaction with what God has already given us.

The apostle Paul illuminated this phenomenon using Israel as an example. He wrote, *"But Israel...failed to reach their goal. And why? Because their minds were fixed on what they achieved instead of on what they believed"* (Romans 9:32 PHILLIPS). What happened to Israel is typical of us all. Without realizing it, we find ourselves relying upon what we have achieved. The Bible says that God resists *"the proud, but gives grace to the humble"* (1 Peter 5:5). It is always His mercy that guides our gaze away from our attainments and back to the knowledge of our need.

Today, church leaders from every stream of Christian thought are beginning to acknowledge their own personal shortcomings. It is dawning upon us that some of the criticisms others have had of our particular group or denomination have had elements of truth. The fact is, we all need correction! And the beginning of that process is found in Jesus resisting our pride and restoring to us fresh hunger to go on.

Thus, in order to ultimately lift Mary higher, Jesus had to lower her opinion of herself: He resisted her on the level she was on. It is interesting that, in response to His resistance, Mary's need to control seemed to have grown more aggressive.

[20] *And He came home, and the multitude gathered again, to such an extent that* [He and His disciples] *could not even eat a meal.*
[21] *And when His own people heard of this, they went out to take custody of Him; for they were saying, "He has lost His senses."* (Mark 3:20–21)

These are strong words here: *"take custody...He has lost His senses."* More than likely, the prevailing influence over Christ's relatives had probably come from Mary. Indeed, in a little while, it would be Mary herself leading them (v. 31). Her unrest had probably caused their unrest. Yet, the issue was not that Jesus has lost His senses, but that they had lost control. Indeed, for Jesus to take control, we must lose control. Revival is as simple as that.

We should be aware that, when the real Christ begins to unveil Himself to His church, He first will reduce us from being leaders to becoming followers again. The very power of Christ to heal, deliver, and work miracles is contained in the revelation of His Lordship. *Deny Him His sovereignty in your church and you deny your church His power*. He will not be manipulated. Remember, Jesus did no miracles until He began to manifest Himself as Lord. From that time on, the only relationships He actively sustained were with those who recognized and submitted to His Lordship over them.

Immediately after learning that Christ's kinsmen came to arrest Him, we read, *"And His mother and His brothers arrived"* (Mark 3:31). We can imagine that, outwardly, Mary was subtly, but clearly, in charge. Inwardly, she was probably troubled and insecure. Jesus, surrounded by a multitude, was told, *"Behold, Your mother and Your brothers are outside looking for You"* (v. 32). The implied undertone of their remark was, "Stop. There is someone here with something more important than what you are now doing." In any other scheme of things, it would be right to honor one's family with special privileges, but not above doing the will of God.

Mary was outside looking in. For what might have been the first time in her life, she felt a spiritual distance between herself and her Son. We should see that the more we set ourselves to control another person, the less intimate we can be with him or her. Intimacy with Jesus will only be found in surrendering to Him, not in controlling Him. Of all those near to Jesus, Mary and her family had slipped the farthest away;

they were outside the sphere of intimate fellowship.

Indeed, when Jesus was told His mother had arrived, He took the opportunity to end this stage of their relationship.

> ³³ *He said, "Who are My mother and My brothers?"*
> ³⁴ *And looking about on those who were sitting around Him, He said, "Behold, My mother and My brothers!*
> ³⁵ *"For whoever does the will of God, he is My brother and sister and mother."* (Mark 3: 33–35)

Though they were outside, they were close enough to hear His rebuke. Right there, the word spoken to Mary thirty years earlier by Simeon was fulfilled: a sword pierced her heart and her inner thoughts were revealed (see Luke 2:35). Christ surgically and mercifully removed from Mary the stronghold of control.

Today, Christ again is removing from us that which seeks to control Him. It was for Mary's good that Jesus ended her tendency to control Him. It was for her gain

that He destroyed that which uncon-
sciously opposed Him. And, it is good that
the Lord cuts off old attitudes and traditions that have limited His freedom to
change us. If we are truly His disciples, we
will not merely survive; we will bear more
fruit under His pruning.

As the day of His return nears, expect
to see many changes. Our destiny is to become the body of Christ with Jesus as the
head. The church was created to receive its
directives from a living relationship with
Him, which would come to us through
seeking Him in prayer and receiving His
word with contriteness of heart.

Christ As Lord over All

Jesus is not being cruel when He ter-
minates our efforts to control Him. Did He
not command us, *"Whoever serves Me must
follow Me"* (John 12:26 NIV)? Yet, with His
command, was there not this promise too,
"and where I am, My servant also will be"
(v. 26)? If we truly follow Him, we will
abide in fellowship with Him. Indeed, His

39

confrontation of us is an answer to our prayers. We have prayed and labored to see the real Jesus emerge through the church—and He is! But, He is coming forth as Lord.

At the same time, this message is not a green light to every rebellious saint who has been waiting to usurp the authority of the pastor; this is not an excuse to justify lawlessness in the church. We are speaking to the leaders and intercessors: if we continue to posture ourselves in prayer, ministering to Jesus as Lord, as did the leaders in Acts 13:1–3, we are going to see the most magnificent demonstrations of God's power and glory.

If we want our Christianity to have Christ, we must let Him rule. Certainly, there will be a thrusting of our lives into greater dependency. Yes, we will be forced to embrace the most drastic of changes. Without doubt, we will be reduced to what seems like the beginnings of our walk with God. Yet, we will also regain the passions of our souls in earnest seeking of the Almighty! How such seeking pleases Him!

Biblically, this new state of heart is called *"first love"* (Revelation 2:4), without which there is no reality of God in our lives. You see, His arms are not short that He cannot reach to our churches and cities. The privilege the Lord is granting us is to enter the most profoundly wonderful, the most unpredictably glorious experience we can have—to know the power of the living God! Reality is filled with meaning in a move of God as dreams are fulfilled in spiritual reality.

However, it is also frightening. There is something about the actual presence of God supernaturally interacting with mankind that has no parallel in mere religion. It is not only a time of power, but also of great carefulness. Not only do the dead come alive, but also the living may, as did Ananias and Sapphira, fall dead. It is the most exultant, yet simultaneously the most fearful thing! Like the women at Christ's tomb, it is a world filled with *"fear and great joy"* (Matthew 28:8). Such is our Christian experience when Jesus is Lord over His church!

What is perhaps most wonderful about serving the Lord is that, even when we fall short, He remains true to His purpose with us. Although His hands wound, they also heal. His correction is not rejection. On the day of Pentecost, Mary and Jesus' brothers are all part of the hundred and twenty in the upper room. The Scriptures specifically mentioned them by name (Acts 1:14).

Mary truly proved to be a bondslave of the Lord. Here was this remarkable woman, humbled and broken, but once again serving God on the highest level of yieldedness. What she had wanted from the beginning she obtained—deep intimacy with Christ. Yet, she reached her goal not by striving or trying to control Jesus, but by her surrender. In the richest way, through the Holy Spirit, Mary again had Jesus living inside her. She learned the secret of how to be, not a controller, but a follower of the Lord Jesus Christ.

4

Current Questions, Timely Answers

*D*uring the past few years we have had several important questions repeatedly asked of us. Hopefully, the following responses will satisfy some areas of debate concerning this current stirring of God.

1. How do you answer people who worry that church unity is a sign of the apostasy, or that praying together is the beginning of the "one-world church"?

It is right to approach these days carefully and with discernment. Jesus warned that, besides wars and natural disasters, the world would see evil released on three major fronts. He said that *"because iniquity shall abound, the love of many shall* [grow] *cold"* (Matthew 24:12). He warned that deception would arise and flood the world with distortion and false doctrines (vv. 11, 24). He said that fear would cause fainting, which would produce inaction and wrong motivations (Luke 21:26). Additionally, the world would see false teachers, false prophets, and false christs all empowered with false signs and wonders (Mark 13:22). Paul called these *"perilous times"* (2 Timothy 3:1). Indeed, they are.

Yet, while we should be cautious, we must not become fearful. In the midst of great apostasy and betrayal, Jesus also stated, *"This gospel of the kingdom shall be preached in the whole world for a witness to all the nations"* (Matthew 24:14). Yes, in spite of increasing deception and darkness, Jesus Himself will guide His church back to the gospel as He taught it. The result will be a most powerful display of Christ's redemptive mercy, a *"witness"* from the very heart of God, *"...and then the end shall come"* (v. 14).

The world will have one final, but legitimate, opportunity to repent before judgment begins. In preparation for this last genuine *"witness"* before the end comes, the Lord is currently cleansing His church. Thus, if we are honestly seeking to do God's will during this sinful, deceptive, and terrifying age, we cannot retreat into fear and overt cautiousness. We must live in purity and honesty, and we must boldly embrace the stature of love typical of saints in God's kingdom. Only by seeking the fullness of Christ's likeness will we be kept from deception, for truth is in Jesus.

The fact is, if we are not motivated by Christ's love toward the other believers in our city, we are already under deception! Just because there will be a false unity in the future, we cannot recoil from true unity today. Nor can we withdraw from Christ's redemptive mercy simply because we are afraid of deception. Indeed, if we are fear-motivated and isolated from other churches, we are already caught in the manipulation and deception of the enemy.

I believe that many who question church unity are sincere. Yet, it amazes me that we have learned to accept rivalry, fault-finding, pride, and prayerlessness as orthodox Christianity—and then criticize pastors who are repenting of sins and praying together! What is most remarkable is that entire congregations actually have been taken in by this deception!

Our safeguard against tomorrow's apostasy is found in today's obedience. God is calling us to humility and repentance, insisting we end our competitive ways. He is requiring that we return to His Word, to love, and to prayer. Today, thousands of leaders in hundreds of cities are seeking God. We are not so much concerned about becoming wrong; we are repenting for the areas that are already wrong in the body of Christ.

2. What will happen if we don't pray?

Perhaps the least ominous consequence to prayerlessness is that nothing will happen. We will stay the way we are— a frightening enough concept in itself! The worst possibility is that conditions around us will so deteriorate that the evil in our cities will become irreversible. Without a major move of God, our nation is lost.

3. Do you see the Lord restoring denominational churches?

Yes! Many denominations began with people who were simply hungry for God. Out of their hunger came fullness and even revival. When we speak of restoration, it is this passion for Jesus that is being restored. Sparked by genuine revivals in key cities, the Holy Spirit will sweep across many nations. Whether entire denominations undergo renewal will depend on the people's passion for God. The promise of the Lord is this: *"Blessed are those who hunger and thirst for righteousness, for they shall be satisfied"* (Matthew 5:6).

4. A number of people see no more than a small harvest at the end of the age. What are your views?

The real question is whether or not there remains one great move of God's Spirit before the return of Christ, for the harvest will be a by-product of a move of God. In answer to this, I will quote the seventeenth-century revivalist, Jonathan Edwards. He wrote,

> We have reason from Scripture prophecy to suppose that, at the commencement of that last and greatest outpouring of the Spirit of God that is to be in the latter ages of the world, the manner of the work will be very extraordinary, and such as never has yet been seen.
>
> (*The Distinguishing Marks of a Work of the Spirit of God*)

Jonathan Edwards believed in at least one great outpouring of God's Spirit before Jesus returns.

The first century church also believed a great harvest would precede Christ's return. Thus, on the day of Pentecost, Peter quoted the prophet Joel concerning the outpouring of the Spirit. But Joel's vision was only partially fulfilled at Pentecost. There yet remains a time of great outpouring, where God grants wonders in the heavens and signs upon the earth *"before the great and glorious day of the Lord shall come"* (Acts 2:20).

The outcome of this display of God's power is that *"everyone who calls on the name of the Lord shall be saved" (Acts 2:21).* This verse was only partially fulfilled at the beginning of this age, yet nations came to Christ during that period! Consider the harvest when the gospel is accompanied by supernatural signs both in the heavens and on earth during its final fulfillment!

Isaiah also tells us that, in the midst of darkness covering the earth and deep darkness the people, the Lord will rise in glory upon His saints (Isaiah 60:2). Because it will be Jesus Himself who is revealed, and not man's ideas or programs, *"nations will come to* [His] *light"* (v. 3).

Our final authority in understanding the size of the harvest is Jesus. He said, *"The harvest is plentiful"* (Matthew 9:37). The problem has always been the lack of laborers: *"but the workers are few"* (v. 37). Where do laborers come from? They are born out of the intercession of the church. Jesus commanded, *"Therefore beseech the Lord of the harvest to send out workers"* (v. 38). This is one of the great cries released during citywide prayer: "God, raise up and send anointed laborers!" It is only the lack of laborers that limits the harvest size, and it is the lack of prayer that limits the effectiveness of God's laborers.

5. Are apostles and prophets being restored to the church?

Because our focus is set upon Jesus, our conferences draw believers from a wide range of views. Some are convinced there were only twelve original apostles, and some can name twelve "apostles" that they know personally. The question challenging us is, How can we unite these people in prayer?

The Lord proved with Saul of Tarsus that He could sovereignly call a man to apostolic ministry. Yet, although Paul had a direct call from the Lord Himself, not until he was commissioned through the praying, citywide leadership in Antioch (see Acts 13:1–3), was he sent out as an apostle. Having seen what God did then reminds us to be humble and flexible now.

However, if apostles are to come forth and function in the church today, they will first be committed to prayer in their cities and be submitted to other local leaders. They will emerge not only sent from God, but from the intercessory womb of the united, praying church (Acts 13:1–3).

What about those today who call themselves apostles? There are a number of leaders around the country who are genuinely doing a foundational work. However, if one is truly called by God to a prophetic or apostolic ministry, he will not be concerned with any title other than *"bondslave of Jesus Christ"* (Colossians 4:12). In fact, the more one insists on being called an apostle or prophet, the less likely it is that he is one.

What we are witnessing is a new beginning born out of prayer and a common desire for Jesus. Our counsel is this: unless the Lord clearly directs otherwise, we should let the praying local church grow with its focus upon Jesus Himself. As relationships mature, the Lord will identify, confirm, and establish each ministry in a harmony of love that will glorify Him and liberate the church.

6. Is there Scripture to doctrinally justify spiritual warfare against principalities and powers?

There is Scripture to justify taking a protective stance when one is under attack from the devil. (See 1 Peter 5:8–9; James 4:7.) And there is scriptural precedent to support times when one is led into spiritual confrontation with the rulers of darkness. (See Luke 4:1–2; Ephesians 6:12.) We err, though, when we take the doctrine of confrontational warfare and make initiatives that are not directly given to us from God and confirmed by the common witness of leaders in the advancing citywide leadership.

It is our belief that the direct confrontation of individuals against principalities and powers cannot be launched from the impulses or initiative of the church; our strategies must come from Christ. (See Jude 1:9.) They must be implemented by leaders and intercessors who are united and anointed in prayer. (See Ephesians 3:10.)

The war in which we are engaged is too broad and complex for a few prayer warriors to succeed alone. The fact is, principalities and powers cannot be cast out from heavenly places the way a demon is driven out of a person. The forces of darkness over a city are not "bound," but displaced by the fullness of Christ in the church.

Doctrinally, the authority of the church over Satan can be found in Luke 10:19, Ephesians 1:19–23, and Ephesians 2:6. As much as it is an error to be fearful of the devil, so it is wrong to move brazenly into warfare. Our counsel is that, ultimately, it takes a citywide church to win the citywide war. Not until a majority of the local church leaders unite in Christ-motivated prayer will Christ's authority be fully released to see the spiritual heavens over their region cleansed of evil. (See 2 Chronicles 7:14; 2 Corinthians 10:6.)

7. How can I unite with other groups ...the Baptists, for instance?

(For the answer to this question, I asked one of the local Baptist pastors, Paul Widen, to share.)

During the recent conference on prayer and revival here in Cedar Rapids, I was approached by several people from around the country who wanted to know how to reach out to their Baptist brethren to invite them for intercession times. There was a great desire to know how to remove the walls that hindered the joining of hearts in prayer. Being a life-long Baptist, I have some idea of the outlook you are confronting. Let me make two simple points.

First, understand that you will not be able to reach all Baptist groups. There are literally hundreds of different Baptist traditions, some of which are "separatist," meaning they avoid contact with the world and other Christian groups they consider suspect. Many of these separatists believe the "show gifts" (tongues, prophesy, even raising your hands in praise!) are not of God, and are either of the flesh or of Satan. Such groups will not normally respond to your invitation.

Second, most Baptists believe Pentecostals look down at them because they do not share the same views concerning the gifting of the Holy Spirit. We have been told we are "incomplete Christians" because we have not spoken in tongues. We even fear worshipping with you because we may be looked down upon for not engaging in the same gifts of the Spirit.

The best way to deal with these issues is to approach your Baptist brethren, after much prayer, with an open heart and a readiness to accept them unconditionally.

When Francis and I met, he had the grace to repent at the outset that Pentecostals had been arrogant in their approach to the gifts of the Spirit. This evoked a strong response in me to listen further. I was moved to repent of the Baptist tendency to box in the Holy Spirit by limiting Him to move and work in only certain, carefully prescribed ways, which is an arrogance that is imbedded in many Baptist traditions.

Francis went on to say the primary gifting of the Holy Spirit is to empower one for holy living, with every other gift of the Spirit being secondary. This point rang a bell in my heart! This is exactly what Baptists have always believed. A bridge was found over which we could cross and meet in fellowship and common purpose. The barriers were gone, and the Holy Spirit did a powerful work in binding us together as brothers.

Repentance, unilateral repentance, broke the initial barriers and made it possible to join hands and hearts in a common purpose, claiming our city and our world for God.

Paul Widen, Pastor
Valley View Baptist Church, Cedar Rapids

8. What is God's plan for Israel?

(To answer this question, I asked Reuven Doron, who is author of *The Children of Promise* and also my dear associate and friend, to respond.)

That a nation would shake off its two thousand-year-old burial cloth, rise from the ashes of the holocaust, and declare itself alive and sovereign is beyond human reasoning and engineering. The big question is whether this phenomenon is of God and, if so, will this "new birth" extend into the promised spiritual reality?

Individual Christians, congregations, and whole denominations are faced with this mystery: can this imperfect, carnal, and as yet unbelieving nation be of God or be instrumental in His hand? And if so, what degree of commitment is the church required to give to Israel?

Many of God's end-time promises and provisions appear to be tightly linked with His work through this resurrected nation. Indeed, much of the anointing that will release certain end-time dynamics in the church will not come until the ancient ingredient of Israel is spiritually restored to the overall unity of the body of Christ.

This much we know: in Isaiah's vision of the coming Messianic kingdom, he saw the following:

> [11] *Then it will happen on that day that the Lord will again recover the second time with His hand The remnant of His people, who will remain...*
> [12] *And He will lift up a standard for the nations, and will assemble the banished ones of Israel, and will gather the dispersed of Judah from the four corners of the earth.* (Isaiah 11:11–12)

Through this particular prophetic telescope, the regathering and reestablishing of national Israel clearly appears as an act of God through which He raises up a *"standard for the nations"* (v. 12). The safest and clearest interpretation of the progressive, though painful, restoration of Israel is that God is making a statement! By His great mercies, the Lord is sending a very real message to the unredeemed, troubled world:

> *Let those who cannot hear God's trumpet nor see God's marvelous work in the church—let them see Israel! Let the blind now see and know for themselves the Sovereign Lord and the integrity of His Word. God speaks to all mankind through Israel, "I, the Lord, change not! What I promise I will perform; and what I require, I shall require still."*

At the very least, Israel is a sign and a standard-bearer of the unfailing character of God's promises.

Reuven Doron, Pastor
River of Life Ministries

The Cities

In 1 Corinthians 10, we learn that God brought Israel into the wilderness to cleanse her of the sins and attitudes of Egypt. Yet, the Lord had an indisputable and glorious goal in His removal of sin: to create an army that would worship Him anywhere—a people who, though differing in gifts and callings, could follow Him and capture cities.

5

When David Captured Jerusalem

One of the great errors of the church is to set its faith and its standards according to yesterday's achievements. Many promises must yet be fulfilled before Jesus returns. Regardless of how widespread the darkness grows, according to Scripture, the Lord's glory is destined to rise upon the purified church.

When it does, *"nations will come to* [its], *light and kings to the brightness of* [His] *rising"* (Isaiah 60:3).

Times of Restoration

The Bible tells us that the last days are not only *"perilous times"* (2 Timothy 3:1 KJV), but also times of renewal and restoration (Acts 3:21). Consequently, we can expect that the frontier of the kingdom of God, in spite of worldwide conflicts, will continually be expanding. Because the Lord's mercies are new every morning (Lamentations 3:22–23), we will see new harvests and new expressions of God's glory and power. Expect to see wonders which our fathers did not see! And trust that what we fail to achieve, our children will attain.

The Blind and the Lame

If King David measured himself by the success of his predecessors, he never would have contemplated an attack against the

Jebusites. The Jebusites were a fierce mountain people and had never been conquered by Israel. In the list of nations to be dispossessed by Jacob, they were always listed last, signifying that victory over the Jebusites would mark the end of one era and herald the advent of another.

Many of Israel's greatest heroes attempted to conquer the Jebusites, but no one, from Joshua to the Judges, had succeeded. (See Joshua 15:63; Judges 1:21.) Thus the Jebusites were contemptuous when they heard of David's plan to possess their chief city, Jerusalem. They mocked Israel's young king: *"You shall not come in here, but the blind and lame shall turn you away"* (2 Samuel 5:6).

There is a lesson here for everyone who desires to see their cities turned toward God. The spiritual forces of evil influencing our communities have heard the boasts and plans of the Christians before us. One can sense the devil's scorn when the church prays for citywide revival. Generally speaking, the church has not succeeded in dislodging the strongholds of wickedness from its cities. The devil's taunts are not without substance, for most of history is on his side.

For the church to succeed in spiritual warfare, God must secure us firmly, not only in the salvation of Christ, but also in the nature of Christ as well. This is for our safety; if our warfare is merely doctrinal in origin, or if it simply comes from our own initiative, it can be perilous. Our hope must rest in Christ, that His presence will both fill and lead us against the citadels of hell.

Why is it that God allows principalities and powers to manipulate people who oppose us? The reason is that this is God's way of securing our souls in Christlikeness. He requires us to bless when we are cursed; when persecuted, to pray; when slandered, to forgive (Luke 6:27–28, 36). By revealing His love through us toward our physical enemies, we are assured that it is His authority speaking through us confronting our spiritual enemies.

The devil's attacks against us often exploit the unbelief, bitterness, and false religious traditions of individuals and churches. We, however, must remain forgiving and not allow the fears and criticisms of others to distract us from our faith. These who oppose the unity of the living church (John 17:21) and its powerful effect of renewing our cities are the modern-day version of *"the blind and lame"* in 2 Samuel 5:6. If we listen to them, they have the potential to *"turn* [us] *away"* from God's will for our lives.

Simply put, the blind do not see that God wants to heal the church and unite us in Jesus. With a forbearing heart, we must realize that the walk of the lame has been hindered by the wounds of life. For whatever reasons, these people still consider division, rivalry, ambition, unforgiveness, and backbiting among congregations to be biblically acceptable.

The blind can hinder our faith by their fears and lack of vision. If we heed the "warnings" of the lame, it is only a matter of time before their woundedness and lack of love will make us as they are—cautious and suspicious. If their opinions influence us, our cities will not be touched by the living, loving body of Christ. Although we definitely need counsel from other Christians, and we certainly must remain forgiving and kind toward those in opposition, we cannot allow the words of the blind and the lame to stop us.

The Fight of Faith

The devil does not come with a trumpet, warning us to prepare for his attack. He comes with subtle and almost reasonable persuasions, as He seeks to dislodge our trust in God. You will recall that, just after the Father spoke to Jesus, *"Thou art My beloved Son..."* (Mark 1:11), Satan attacked the Lord's faith: *"If You are the Son..."* (Matthew 4:3). The word of God to Christ was immediately challenged by the devil.

When Satan comes through the pseudo-spiritual, doubt-laden advice of *"the blind and lame,"* we can be more beguiled and hesitant than had the devil directly confronted us in a bold, frontal assault.

When David Captured Jerusalem

Like never before, God needs people with faith. When Jesus came to bring revival and healing to His hometown, *"He did not do many miracles there because of their unbelief"* (Matthew 13:58). When the Lord called the official's daughter back from death, Jesus first put the mockers and unbelievers outside (Matthew 9:25). Likewise, when God puts a dream in your heart, whether it is a holy desire for your city or any other vision, you also must put the mockers and unbelievers outside. You alone are responsible for your fulfilling God's will for your life.

We should expect the word of the Lord to be resisted, even by our own carnal minds! Regardless of the onslaught, like Paul, we must not be *"disobedient to the heavenly vision"* (Acts 26:19). Our fight is *"the good fight of faith"* (1 Timothy 6:12); and faith is not just believing there is a God (James 2:19), it is believing what God has said (Romans 4:20–21). As it is written:

³ *The vision is yet for the appointed time; it hastens toward the goal, and it will*

69

> *not fail. Though it tarries, wait for it; for*
> *it will certainly come, it will not delay.*
> [4] *Behold, as for the proud one, his soul*
> *is not right within him; but the right-*
> *eous will live by his faith.*
>
> (Habakkuk 2:3–4)

To *"live by...faith"* is to believe God until the vision He gave you comes to pass.

We follow the living Christ, not merely a moral code. It is the Lord Himself who has stirred our hearts! In daily prayer, in confirmation of the sacred Scriptures, and through dreams and visions, the Lord of Hosts is speaking to His church. He is calling His people to war. His immediate goal is to see His church revived and then see our cities healed.

David believed God and, in spite of history being on the side of the Jebusites, *"Nevertheless, David captured the stronghold of Zion, that is the city of David"* (2 Samuel 5:7). David conquered the stronghold of the Jebusites and called it the city of David. And then he made a decree: *"The blind or the lame shall not come into the house"* (v. 8).

The Word of God Is Our Leader!

When King David heard the taunts of the Jebusites, he did not draw back in unbelief, nor was his faith crushed because of his ancestors' failures. David interpreted the battle in light of the promises of God. At stake was the integrity of the Lord's personal promise to Abraham and to his seed: *"Your descendants will take possession of the cities of their enemies"* (Genesis 22:17 NIV). While the enemy may have had history on his side, David had the unalterable word of God on his side!

The heritage of Abraham's spiritual offspring is to bring the prevailing influence of God into their communities and, through Christ, "possess" cities. It is a reproach that the devil wants our cities more than the church does! David's desire for Jerusalem was a godly desire that came to him from Christ, for what outwardly was to become David's city was soon to become the city of God.

As David simply believed God's promises, so we must also. What has God said concerning our cities? Many pastors, upon entering the ministry, heard the Lord whisper inwardly to them, *"I have given you this city."* Sadly, Satan has them convinced that the voice was not God's. Yet, the Lord has not only promised us cities, He has sworn that *"nations will come to your light"* (Isaiah 60:3). Indeed, the Father Himself appeals to the Spirit of Christ in us, *"Ask of Me, and I will surely give the nations as Thine inheritance"* (Psalm 2:8).

Whom should we believe? The lame? They are not walking with God. The blind? They do not see what we see. Let us take God at His Word. Jesus Himself assures us, *"All things are possible to him who believes"* (Mark 9:23). If we fail, we join the ranks of the spiritual heroes who *"died in faith, without receiving the promises"* (Hebrews 11:13). In truth, it is better to die in faith than to live in doubt.

But consider this: What if we succeed? What if, through the process of believing God, He imparts to us Christ's character and empowers us to see our cities healed? What if it is time for the Jebusites to fall?

The Anointing of David

God cannot lay claim upon a city before He lays claim upon our hearts. His plan is a man, anointed and raised up to serve the purposes of God in his generation. Concerning David, the Lord said, *"Since the day that I brought My people Israel from Egypt, I did not choose a city out of all the tribes of Israel in which to build a house that My name might be there, but I chose David"* (1 Kings 8:16). Significantly, Jerusalem is called *"the city of David"* 46 times in the Bible, while it is called the *"city of God"* only four times (Psalm 46:4; 48:1, 8; 87:3). As far as this world is concerned, Jerusalem was David's before it became God's.

In our day, God's anointing for our cities may initially rest upon one and spread to others, or come simultaneously upon several and then grow. Ultimately, the Lord will raise up spiritual leaders in the city who will be united without jealousy or fear among them.

David and those who led Israel with him respected the call and anointing of

God on one another. David was ordained as king, Nathan and Gad as prophets, and Zadok as priest. Along with the other prophets, priests, and David's *"mighty men"* (2 Samuel 10:7), they were remarkably free of rivalry and ambition.

Motivating and sustaining them throughout their lives, from the wilderness to the palace, was a deep, prevailing sense of awe toward God. They were worshippers of the living God. Characteristic of David's heart is the fact that, when David first fled from Saul, David did not bring his sword, but rather he took his harp. (See 1 Samuel 21:8; Psalm 57:8 and subheading). After he captured Jerusalem, David commissioned singers and musicians to continually praise and worship God. Worship of God was the infrastructure of David's success in warfare.

Additionally, all of these men were probably within a few years of each other in age. (See 1 Kings 1.) They were a generation who, although they came from differing backgrounds, became friends and comrades. They obtained the promises of

God that were left to them by Joshua and Israel's other generals.

We are also called to secure what our forefathers did not attain, to live in faith for what God has promised:

> [2] *For behold, darkness will cover the earth, and deep darkness the peoples; but the LORD will rise upon you, and His glory will appear upon you.*
> [3] *And nations will come to your light, and kings to the brightness of your rising.* (Isaiah 60:2–3)

6

The
Deliverers

*I*n the midst of worldwide conflict, we must not lose the focus of God upon our cities. How will the Lord answer our cry for our cities? How will deliverance come? In response to the prayers and repentance of His people, the Lord shall raise up deliverers, individuals and teams of individuals who are anointed to liberate their churches and cities from darkness.

Repentance Precedes Revival

Revival does not just happen. Certain spiritual conditions must reside in the human heart before the Lord visits His people. Throughout the Scriptures we see an ongoing pattern: in response to the prayers and suffering of His people, the Lord raises up deliverers, individuals who are spiritually empowered to defeat Israel's oppressors.

It is important to note that the effectiveness of these deliverers was never based upon their own worthiness or credentials. Although they were sent by God, their arrival was synchronized with Israel's repentance. As Israel cried out to God, deliverers were raised up and anointed with the power of the Holy Spirit.

Nehemiah spoke of this process in his prayer before God. He prayed,

> [27] *Therefore Thou didst deliver them into the hand of their oppressors who oppressed them, but when they cried to Thee in the time of their distress, Thou*

> *didst hear from heaven, and according*
> *to Thy great compassion Thou didst*
> *give them deliverers who delivered*
> *them from the hand of their oppressors.*
> (Nehemiah 9:27)

When the people of Israel turned away from the Lord, they were soon delivered into the hand of their enemies. This led to *"the time of their distress"* when they cried to the Lord. God heard and, in answer to their prayers, sent to them *"deliverers who delivered them from the hand of their oppressors."*

We see this pattern in the book of Exodus, when the Lord first called Moses. The Redeemer said,

> [7] *I have surely seen the affliction of My*
> *people who are in Egypt, and have*
> *given heed to their cry because of their*
> *taskmasters, for I am aware of their*
> *sufferings.*
> [8] *So I have come down to deliver them*
> *from the power of the Egyptians, and to*
> *bring them up from that land to a good*
> *and spacious land, to a land flowing*
> *with milk and honey...* (Exodus 3:7–8)

Notice that the Lord saw the affliction of His people; He heard their cries; He knew their sufferings. God is never far from the plight of mankind. In a similar situation, we read that the Lord *"could bear the misery of Israel no longer"* (Judges 10:16). Even though many of the pains of the people of God are because of their sins, still the Lord bears the misery of His people. Their distresses distress Him; their suffering becomes His suffering; their cries are the catalyst for His divine intervention.

In our text in Exodus, we observe that God not only heard their prayers, but also their cries. It is one thing to pray about a need, but quite another to weep over it. Those who mourn are comforted (Matthew 5:4). The Lord knew their afflictions and their sufferings. God sends anointed deliverers in answer to a constant cry.

Perhaps the Lord has not fully answered us because we are not yet desperate enough to draw out His compassions. Our prayer is still comfortably contained within a schedule. It is not a constant, *"day and night"* (Luke 18:7) cry that unceasingly comes before God. While troubled, we are not afflicted by the conditions of our society; though saddened, we are not weeping with those who weep (Romans 12:15).

A few believers truly have surrendered to the vulnerability of Christ's compassion. They bear in their intercession not only the need of the people, but their pain as well. These intercessors are laying down their reputations, their jobs, their very lives to see the sins of our society cleansed. Still a minority, they carry in their souls the anguish of their cities. They hear the cry of the oppressed; they know the suffering of the afflicted. God is ready to respond to their prayer. Out of their midst He shall raise up and anoint deliverers. At the proper time, such people will be empowered to bring healing to their cities.

We Must Want Deliverance, Not Just Relief

Ministries today attempt to deliver people who have neither cried for help nor repented. Those they pray for may receive a short, limited blessing, but soon they return to sin and oppression. Although there are exceptions to this rule, we must discern if an individual is ready to be released before we minister deliverance. Are they repentant? Have they put away their idols? Is their heart truly turning toward God?

This pattern for the individual is also God's pattern for the church and its city. As the Lord did not deliver Israel until its people cried for help, so the war for our churches and cities will not be won until a significant number of the people are crying in prayer to God. Is not God's purpose in the praying, citywide church to develop the heart attitudes to which He can respond? Without the substructure of prayer and crying before God, deliverance, binding and loosing, and other forms of spiritual warfare are significantly limited. Deliverance is the final stage of corporate repentance.

Long-term strategies for the renewal of our cities require not only an anointed people, but the anointed time. The focus of the Lord is to turn the citywide church to prayer. Without the cry of the church to heaven, there will not be the response of heaven leading to revival.

Looking again to the Scriptures, we read,

> [9] *And when the sons of Israel cried to the LORD, the LORD raised up a deliverer for the sons of Israel to deliver them, Othniel the son of Kenaz, Caleb's younger brother.*
> [10] *And the Spirit of the LORD came upon him, and he judged Israel…*
> (Judges 3:9–10)

And again we find,

> [15] *But when the sons of Israel cried to the LORD, the LORD raised up a deliverer for them, Ehud the son of Gera, the Benjamite, a left-handed man….*
> (Judges 3:15)

The key in these and many other Scriptures regarding deliverers is that, preceding their arrival, the people of Israel *"cried to the LORD."* Likewise, the church must cry out to God before the anointing comes for doing successful warfare.

Often years of being oppressed and crying out to God preceded the Lord's action. The praying church should not put a timetable upon the length of their commitment to intercession. God desires full dedication. If the length of time required to bring change hinders us, the preparatory work is not yet deep enough to draw the Lord's response. To see our cities turned toward God, we must simply pray until it happens.

The Nature of Deliverers

Gideon exemplifies the spiritual traits of deliverers and the anointing upon them. To be sure, such individuals were only raised up when evil and oppression covered the land. The ministry of deliverance was always birthed out of a womb of social darkness.

> [7] *Now it came about when the sons of Israel cried to the LORD on account of Midian,*
> [8] *that the LORD sent a prophet to the sons of Israel...* (Judges 6:7–8)

The future deliverance of Israel began with the sons of Israel crying to the Lord; the Lord responded to them with a prophetic word. The prophetic anointing does more than teach: it proclaims the intention of God, confronts strongholds of sin in the people, and prepares society for an outpouring of the Spirit.

In this case, the prophet was not the deliverer. He simply reminded Israel of former deliverances. He reiterated God's command of many generations: *"I am the LORD your God; you shall not fear the gods of the Amorites in whose land you live"* (Judges 6:10).

The *"gods of the Amorites"* were the demonic principalities and powers that ruled the countries in Canaan. The idols erected to these evil spirits were physical symbols of spiritual bondage. Paul instructed us that when people honor an idol, *"they sacrifice to demons"* (1 Corinthians 10:20). The Lord commanded Israel not to fear these demon gods. The Hebrew word *yare,* which is translated as *"fear,"* means "to reverence; to live in an intellectual or

The Deliverers

emotional anticipation of harm." We will never be victorious over the enemy if we live in dread of his retaliation.

Great wisdom must be exercised in spiritual warfare. No one should engage in battle against the powers of darkness with a flippant or casual attitude. An even greater error is committed when we are afraid of the enemy. Indeed, we are commanded not to fear the gods of the Amorites (or the "spirit-gods" over our cities). If a Christian teacher instructs you to fear principalities and powers, you must not fear what he fears. You should respect the power of evil spirits, but it is sin to live in fear of them. When the Lord gave us authority *"over all the power of the enemy,"* He promised, *"nothing shall injure you"* (Luke 10:19).

First, the prophet warned Israel not to fear the Canaanite gods. Then, the Lord set Himself to deliver Israel of fear. God always begins the deliverance of the many with the deliverance of one. The angel of the Lord found Gideon hiding from the Midianites. His greeting is astounding:

"The Lord is with you, O valiant warrior"
(Judges 6:12).

The Lord may take years to prepare a servant, but when the Lord unsheathes His sword, He moves quickly. God wasted no time in establishing the man of His choosing, calling him by his future identity, *"valiant warrior."*

Gideon, no doubt, wondered that he was the valiant warrior to whom the angel spoke. This is the first aspect of the deliverer's nature: he is surprised, even shocked, that the Lord has called him! He has no secret wish to be a hero, no hidden ambition for prominence. He is not even a "natural-born" leader.

Perhaps in Gideon's fear, he imagined another *"valiant warrior"* near him of whom he was previously unaware. There is a Mighty Warrior in us of whom we, too, are unaware. His name is the Lord of Hosts, and greater is He who is in us than he who is in the world (1 John 4:4). As our thoughts conform to His, the Lord's anointing will come forth through us in the timing of God.

In this first encounter, Gideon asks the Lord a very legitimate question:

> [13] *O my lord, if the LORD is with us, why then has all this happened to us? And where are all His miracles which our fathers told us about, saying, "Did not the LORD bring us up from Egypt?"*
> (Judges 6:13)

Everyone who sincerely seeks the endorsement of God must ask this question: Why does it seem as though the Lord has abandoned us? We must question the apparent distance between us and heaven, for the answers reveal our need of repentance.

God has not left His people; the question is superfluous. The Lord has initiated the encounter, and the time of separation is past. His miracles are about to begin!

> [14] *And the LORD looked at him and said, "Go in this your strength and deliver Israel from the hand of Midian. Have I not sent you?"* (Judges 6:14)

Gideon was the youngest in his father's house, and his family was the least in

Manasseh. What strength has he? How will Gideon deliver Israel? The strength of God's servants is in their commission from the Lord. *"Have I not sent you?"* (v. 14) Having been sent by God, we go in His authority. This is the next spiritual stage in God's raising up a deliverer. He is commissioned and sent by the Lord.

Jesus gave to His disciples the same basic appointment Gideon received, *"As Thou didst send Me into the world, I also have sent them into the world"* (John 17:18). Those whom the Lord sends, He empowers. As we obey, all we need to accomplish our task will be provided.

At this point, Gideon's eyes were opened, and he saw God. Fearing death, he cried out concerning his own unworthiness,

[22] *Alas, O Lord GOD! For now I have seen the angel of the LORD face to face.*
[23] *And the LORD said to him, "Peace to you, do not fear; you shall not die."*

(Judges 6:22–23)

Gideon built an altar to the Lord and called it, *"The LORD is Peace"* (v. 24). No one can truly stand against the enemy if he is unsure of his standing before God. And this is the third qualification for the deliverer: he has peace with God. Before the Lord sends His servants forth, they must know the power of His blood, the forgiveness of their sins, and their justification by faith. Whenever they look toward heaven, they must know, *"The LORD is Peace."*

Ourselves, Our Families, and Our Cities!

> [25] *The LORD said to him, "...pull down the altar of Baal which belongs to your father, and cut down the Asherah that is beside it;*
> [26] *"and build an altar to the LORD your God on the top of this stronghold in an orderly manner...."* (Judges 6:25–26)

The same night that the Lord revealed Himself to Gideon, He sent him forth to pull down the altar of Baal that belonged to his father. It is important to note that the victory of the Lord was brought forth *"in an orderly manner."*

Keep this in mind: after the Lord delivered Gideon, He sent him to pull down the strongholds in his family. This is the fourth aspect of the nature of the Lord's deliverers: their families will be in order. The deliverers will be anointed to bring order. This will first be manifested in their own hearts, then in their families, and finally in their cities.

The battle for our cities begins by pulling down the strongholds of the enemy that have infiltrated our own lives. It continues by bringing our immediate families into prayer and order. While there are exceptions to this rule, it is generally true that if we disregard the vulnerability of our family to satanic assault, the enemy will have many open doors to undermine and hinder God's work.

Pulling down a stronghold is only half the battle. On the very site where the enemy once was worshipped, we must now build an altar to the Lord. If the stronghold was fear, we replace it with an altar of faith. If it was bitterness, love must take its place. On the level of a city or a region, where perversion ruled, purity must now be built. Where greed once triumphed, generosity must now reign.

When Gideon pulled down his father's altar to Baal and build one to God (Judges 6:27–28), instead of being welcomed and applauded by the people of Ophah, they came as a group to kill him (v. 30)! The demonic power that ruled the area now stirred its captives to oppose the Lord's servant! However, Gideon's father defended his son and said, *"If* [Baal] *is a god, let him contend for himself"* (v. 31). Be aware that those whose thoughts are sympathetic with the evil a deliverer has come to destroy will rise up to defend the enemy! Expect resistance, even among God's people!

By common consent it was decided to rename Gideon, "Jerubbaal," which meant, "Let Baal contend against him." In the Bible a name change signified a change of nature as well. Gideon went from being a fearful captive to a fearless captain. And perhaps this is the last dimension of the deliverer: having been sent by the Lord with His anointing, a deliverer mobilizes

God's people to face their enemies and conquer them.

The Lord is raising up deliverers in answer to the prayers and cries of His people. As we travel throughout the nations we see individuals laying down their lives to draw the church together in repentance and prayer. From among these will come individuals and teams of individuals whose anointing and power meet the needs of our times. They will be sent by God. They will not come to "try" anything; they will come to carry out the expressed will of God. What they decree will come to pass. They will lead a repentant people out of oppression and into the victory of the Lord!

Let us pray:

Father, draw us together in our cities to pray. Allow our souls to feel the desperate condition of the people. Forgive us our lust for comfort. Make us a house of prayer. Lord, raise up deliverers for Your glory! Amen.

7

America's Future: Christ or Chaos

*T*here is a chosen race. From **"every nation and tribe and tongue and people"** (Revelation 14:7), they have been purchased by the Lamb, united by His blood, and chosen to reveal His glory. Their homeland is the kingdom of God, and the redemption they have found in Christ is God's answer for ethnic strife and conflicts.

93

Exodus of the Gentiles

While the return of the Jews to Israel is this century's most remarkable exodus, it is not the only restoration of ethnic peoples in recent years. Indeed, Israel's restoration is but one of hundreds of ethnic groups who are resurfacing in today's world, each clothed in the individuality of its ancient heritage.

In this "Gentile Exodus," nations are returning not only to their native identities but, like Israel, many are reclaiming their original homelands as well. From the cessation of colonialism in African, Asian, and the Middle Eastern countries to the emergence of dozens of ethnic peoples at the fall of communism, nations are returning to their ethnic ancestry.

"Indeed, My decision is to gather nations, to assemble kingdoms..." (Zephaniah 3:8). God has placed a desire in man to return to his origins. The separation of Czechoslovakia into two ethnic peoples and the restoration of Germany into one nation has come by a decree from above.

It is easy for us as Americans to boast in our victory in the war with Iraq, but it was the Almighty's decision to preserve ethnic identities, not merely American technology, which has delivered the Kuwaitis and is prodding the Kurds toward autonomy. And, it was the influence of the Lord of Hosts, not only the United Nations, who, after the Gulf War, preserved the sovereignty of the Iraqis.

Never in history has there been a time when nations and peoples were so universally drawn toward their ancestral distinctions. Incredibly, since World War II there have been over 100 new republics established, fully sixty percent of all nations; and most of these were secured through warfare and bloodshed. In the last fifty years more national identities and borders were replaced than were changed by all the previous wars in history.

Yet, awakening simultaneously with these new nations, as though foreign occupation were but a dream in the night, are ancient hatreds and conflicts. And it is where neighboring peoples have occupied the same land during different eras, as with the breakup of Yugoslavia, that the fires of ethnic and racial clashes are most consuming.

Jesus warned His disciples of this day, saying, *"nation will rise against nation"* (Matthew 24:7). Indeed, it should be no surprise that, in the original language of the Scriptures, the Greek word for "nation" is *ethnos*, from which we derive our word "ethnic." Christ foresaw that ethnic conflicts, racially-based violence, and religious wars would reach unparalleled heights at the consummation of this age.

America: A Nation of Nations

One has only to look at the Los Angeles riots to forecast where America's ethnic problems are taking us. Consider that noticeably missing from the news coverage of plundered grocery and department stores were the area's gangs. Where were they? They had pillaged the gun and sporting goods stores. Thousands of weapons were stolen during the riots by gang members. This is especially significant as there are 70,000 gang members in Los Angeles but only 10,000 police.

Most Americans were shocked at the video tape of the Rodney King beating, but what Americans witnessed for the first time on television was simply a reenactment of the way dominant social groups historically have handled minorities. In fact, since civilization began, it has typically been repressive forms of police or military action which contained ethnic unrest and rebellion. In the former Soviet Union, social unrest was always firmly and quickly crushed. Although most American law enforcers do not practice cruel police tactics, a significant number are sympathetic with the thinking that justifies it.

Nearly every nation with ethnic communities has, at some time or another, had to resort to severe methods of restraint to restore order. But these forms of aggressive containment are, themselves, being handcuffed by their exposure to worldwide public opinion.

With a sober eye let us realize that, apart from a revival of pure Christianity (not just Christian traditions, but eternal heavenly values), there will never be lasting remedies for racial injustice before Jesus comes. In fact, the Lord warned about these very days. He said that nation will rise against nation, ethnic group against ethnic group. Recall also that America, the "melting pot" of the world, is a nation of nations.

Racial Conflicts and the Kingdom of God

One thing we must not do, however, is to allow ourselves to be moved by fear or unbelief. Increased wars, lawlessness, and ethnic conflicts are signs that point to something more significant than themselves. Jesus said, *"Even so you, too, when you see these things happening, recognize that the kingdom of God is near"* (Luke 21:31). Indeed, the turbulence we behold in the sea of humanity is caused by a storm in the heavenly places: *"the kingdom of heaven is at hand"* (Matthew 4:17)! The signs around us are actually effects of a confrontation between the kingdom of God and the domain of hell.

And while ethnic peoples are struggling toward their ancient identities, so there is another people, drawn out from every nation and tribe and tongue who, in their hearts and minds, are returning to their homeland—the kingdom of God. For while great pressure is being exerted upon nations to exalt their ethnicity, so also there is a return in the true church to the purity and power of our origins in Christ. Like no other time in history, our identity in Christ must be greater, more compelling, more real to us, than any natural bonding we have in the world.

Remember, it was in this very context of international upheaval that Jesus said, *"And this gospel of the kingdom shall be preached in the whole world for a witness to all the nations, and then the end shall come"* (Matthew 24:14).

Why did Jesus speaking of the gospel of the kingdom being preached at the end of the age? The answer is at least twofold. First, we proclaim the kingdom because it truly will be *"at hand"* (Matthew 10:7). In His great mercy God is going to give all nations one last legitimate opportunity to choose, not merely between the church and the world, but between heaven or hell. The nations will be given a *"witness"* of heaven, *"and then the end shall come."* Those who call upon the Lord will become part of the Great Harvest. Those who reject Him, however, will have become so hardened, they will earn for themselves the fierceness of God's wrath.

God's second motive in calling for the proclamation of His kingdom is to spare His people from ethnic violence. He seeks to guide us out of our individual ethnic mentality into the eternal life of His kingdom, for the kingdom of God is free from racism and cultural pride. Indeed, if the Christians of opposing ethnic peoples humble themselves and unite in prayer, and if, instead of allowing offenses to escalate, they confess their sins and forgive each other, they will preserve themselves and their communities during this time of great upheaval.

It is vital for us, as Christ's church, to return to what Jesus called the *"gospel of the kingdom."* What is this message? It is the teaching of Christ. It is more penetrating than our typical salvation message; the gospel of the kingdom makes disciples, not just converts. It is more demanding than the prosperity gospel, for this, truly, will cost you everything. But while the gospel of the kingdom requires more, it gives more; it is the gospel as Jesus lived it, full of power, love, and reconciliation. And its good news is not simply that someday we will go to heaven, but that heaven is coming to us.

One Answer for Ethnic Clashes

The pressures that ultimately thrust the world into accepting the antichrist and his government will not eradicate ethnicity among the peoples. Beneath the surface of a one-world government, ethnic cultures will remain intact and in conflict with one another. This is an unending judgment that God Himself uttered at mankind's first attempt at ethnic unity—ancient Babylon. The Lord decreed that, apart from uniting in Him, men *"will not understand each other"* (Genesis 11:7 NIV).

There are too many wounds, too many ancient, unreconciled conflicts, too long a history of injustice, hatreds, and fears for mankind to unite apart from the forgiveness of Christ. In describing these last days, especially the last kingdom on earth, Daniel revealed an intriguing fact: *"It will be a divided kingdom"* (Daniel 2:41). Although the people of the kingdom will be divided, *"they will combine with one another in the seed of men; but they will not adhere to one another"* (v. 43).

Daniel said, *"They will combine with one another in the seed of men..."* At the end of the age, ethnic issues will continue to compel mankind to extreme remedies, even uniting the seed of men (genetic engineering?). The word that is translated *"seed"* means "offspring, family, race." Humanistic mankind will do everything possible to deal with ethnic crises, but, as Daniel continued, *"...they will not adhere to one another."*

There will be no solution offered to mankind's racial and ethnic problems apart from Christ in the kingdom of God. However, Daniel had more to say concerning the future. Directly linked to his prophecy of man's divided kingdom, Daniel also revealed:

> [44] *And in the days of those kings the God of heaven will set up a kingdom which will never be destroyed, and that kingdom will not be left for another people; it will crush and put an end to all these kingdoms, but it will itself endure forever.* (Daniel 2:44)

Daniel spoke of an unprecedented time at the end of the age, a time when *"the people that do know their God shall be strong, and do exploits"* (Daniel 11:32 KJV). Both Jesus and Daniel spoke of the kingdom of God beginning to be displayed while the world experiences ethnic and geophysical conflicts.

As the Church Becomes
God's Kingdom

The United States government began its first real effort to deal with racial injustice in the 1960s. Since then about three trillion dollars worth of changes have been implemented. And while much good occurred, sociologists tell us that, for many African-Americans, conditions have actually worsened since the early 1970s.

Before we spend another trillion dollars on irreconcilable ethnic problems, we, the church, need to see how God's kingdom is already influencing the church. Today we are seeing thousands of pastors and intercessors from nearly every church and ethnic background being reconciled to each other. God is doing what man cannot do. He is healing the nations, the *ethnos*. Together, they are beginning to manifest the kingdom of God.

This is what was revealed to John:

[9] *Worthy art Thou to take the book, and to break its seals; for Thou wast slain,*

> *and didst purchase for God with Thy*
> *blood men from every tribe and tongue*
> *and people and nation.*
> [10] *And Thou hast made them to be a*
> *kingdom and priests to our God; and*
> *they will reign upon the earth.*
>
> (Revelation 5:9–10)

Each month we receive letters and articles from many places where this healing is occurring in the church. Again, we read in Malachi, *"But for you who fear My name the sun of righteousness will rise with healing in its wings..."* (Malachi 4:2). From Memphis we read of white pastors repenting to black ministers for the sins of racism and slavery committed against blacks on Auction Street. In Kansas City, Christian leaders united with Native Americans and African-Americans; again, repentance and reconciliation occurred. All over the world God is establishing the preliminary stage of His kingdom, repentance and reconciliation.

Indeed, it is here in the church where the healing of our society has always begun; and it is here where it will occur again at the end of this age. God is calling us from every color and background to unite in Him as His family and His kingdom. As every nation can be traced back ultimately to a father, so our lineage as Christians begins with our common ancestry God is our Father.

Is there a chosen race? Yes. As citizens of His kingdom, we *"are a chosen race, a royal priesthood, a holy nation..."* (1 Peter 2:9). We are a race of every color, a people whose father is God and whose homeland is the kingdom of heaven.

8

The Timeless Wisdom of Martin Luther King, Jr.

*A*s the waves of ethnic unrest continue to swell, we need the wisdom
of Martin Luther King. Although
he was a man sent by God, sadly, too many
of the white community know more about
what his accusers have said than what Dr.
King actually believed. Even if their criticisms were legitimate, remember that
David sinned, but we still read the Psalms.

Whites need to hear Brother King's heart. The black community needs to recall his message. And all of us need to return to it.

Quotes from Dr. King:

Recognizing the necessity for suffering, I have tried to make of it a virtue. If only to save myself from bitterness, I have attempted to see my personal ordeals as an opportunity to transform myself and heal the people involved in the tragic situation which now remains. I have lived these last few years with the conviction that unearned suffering is redemptive. There are some who still find the cross a stumbling block, and others consider it foolishness, but I am more convinced than ever before that it is the power of God unto social and individual salvation.

—*Pilgrimage to Nonviolence*
April 1960

In the final analysis, says the Christian ethic, every man must be respected because God loves him. The worth of an individual does not lie in the measure of his intellect, his racial origin, or his social position. Human worth lies in relatedness to God. An individual has value because he has value to God. Whenever this is recognized, "whiteness" and "blackness" pass away as determinants in a relationship, and "son" and "brother" are substituted.

—*The Ethical Demands*
December 1962

We have before us the glorious opportunity to inject a new dimension of love into the veins of our civilization. There is still a voice crying out in terms that echo across the generations, saying: Love your enemies, bless them that curse you, pray for them that despitefully use you, that you may be the children of your Father which is in Heaven...This love might well be the salvation of our civilization...

—*Facing the Challenge of a New Day*
December 1956

I have a dream that one day every valley shall be exalted, every hill and mountain shall be made low, the rough places shall be made plain and the crooked places shall be made straight and the glory of the Lord will be revealed and all flesh shall see it together. This is our hope. This is the faith that I go back to the South with. With this faith we will be able to hew out of the mountain of despair a stone of hope. With this faith we will be able to transform the jangling discords of our nation into a beautiful symphony of brotherhood. With this faith we will be able to work together, to pray together...

—*I Have a Dream*
August 1963

The preceding quotes were taken from *A Testament of Hope,* edited by James M. Washington.

The
Covenant

For all we think depends upon us, in truth, the church exists because of the conversations between the Father and His Son. Our confidence in prayer, in faith, and in our future rests upon the sovereignty of God and the integrity of the Father's promise to His Son.

9

Those Who Make a Covenant with God

*I*n talking with national and international prayer leaders, I find many are
hearing a similar word: the Lord is
calling His people to unite with Him in
covenant power for our nation!

The Covenant-Keeping God

Throughout the history of God's dealings with man, He has revealed Himself as a covenant-making God. The Almighty covenanted with Noah, Abraham, Moses, and David; He renewed His Abrahamic covenant in His call to Isaac and Jacob. Each covenant initiated a new wave of redemptive power into the world and forever impacted the human condition.

The word *covenant* means "to fetter" or "to chain together." It was the highest form of commitment that two individuals could share. Any of several rituals were employed to express the covenant partners' unity. A sword might be passed, signifying that the two would be united against the enemy as one. They might pass a sandal between themselves, which symbolized they would travel any distance to be at one another's side. Or, they might cut an animal in two and pass between its halves. As each half, though separated, was still one animal, so the two covenant partners would become as one individual.

When the Lord initiated His covenant with a man, He did so as an extension of His eternal purpose. The man was a component in a series of divine initiatives. Contained within the Lord's covenant were His divine intervention, His supernatural wisdom and strategies, and His provision.

Thus, if we look at the Lord's call to Noah, we see that it was not the ark, but the covenant of God, that preserved Noah and his family during worldwide judgment. Noah was a component, a factor in a series of divine initiatives, that accomplished the Lord's predetermined plans. God established the covenant, designed the ark, and brought the animals. The Lord even shut the door after Noah entered the ark.

When the Lord established His covenant with Abraham, He appeared as a flaming torch. Twice the torch of God passed through the halves of the animals Abraham had offered in sacrifice. The two passes signified that God would keep His part of the covenant and He would keep Abraham's part of the covenant as well! Today, a restored Israel testifies to God's faithfulness in His covenant with Abraham, Isaac, and Jacob. And it is God, not merely the Jewish military, that preserves Israel in our times.

The agreement the Lord cut with His covenant partner upheld not only His servant, but His servant's descendants as well. Noah and his family, Abraham and his seed, Moses and Israel, all were united as beneficiaries of God's covenant relationship. Similarly, we are saved and sustained through life's battles by Christ's covenant with the Father, of which the cross was the consummate and most glorious act of our redemption.

Payment and Pattern

It is vital for us to see that our salvation has been secured, not only because Jesus died for our sins, but because His death was part of a covenant He had with the Father. The fact that Jesus suffered on my behalf is staggering, but His crucifixion was a component of the more powerful reality of His covenant with the Father.

The terms of Christ's covenant were such that, if He would live His life blamelessly and offer that holy life upon the cross for sins, then everyone who looked to Jesus would be granted forgiveness. The Father would look to Christ's sacrifice for justice, and sinners would look to Jesus for mercy. Just as Noah's family was saved through the flood, so we, through Christ's covenant with the Father, are saved and delivered from the judgments of God upon this world.

Yet, as maturing disciples, we find in Christ's covenant mission not only our peace, but also a pattern Christ calls us to follow. He told His disciples, *"As the Father has sent Me, I also send you"* (John 20:21). Having laid down His life in covenant surrender, He now bids us, *"take up [your] cross, and follow Me"* (Matthew 16:24).

Of course, we will never supersede Christ's covenant. However, by picking up our own cross, we are called to extend the redemptive power of Christ's cross into our world and times. Jesus' covenant is an eternal pact. For it to be revealed in time, the Lord calls us to follow Him in personal covenants for our homes, cities, and nations.

The covenant we embrace is nothing less than the expansion of Christ's nature, revealed once again through the obedience and love of His disciples. In this act of laying down our lives for our cities, we follow Jesus into the same life that He exemplified in dying for the sins of the world.

The Harvest and Covenant Power

To many Christians, the idea of making a special covenant with God is unfamiliar. Yet, I believe that many have already felt the Holy Spirit speaking, urging them to deepen their commitment to Christ. Even so, covenants and our obedience to them must come from our hearts in response to the Lord's initiative. You will know the extent of your covenant by the measure of vision and faith God provides.

Especially in the last days, we need to become a people who know the truth that is given to us through Christ's covenant. And, in following Him, we should also know the unique endowment of grace He brings in making special covenants with us.

Indeed, Daniel 11:28–32 warns that the last days will be a time of unprecedented deception and spiritual intrigue. According to this text, Satan's rage will be hurled uniquely against *"the holy covenant"* (v. 28). Yet, in this very same passage of Daniel, we read,

> [32] *And by smooth words he will turn to godlessness those who act wickedly toward the covenant, but the people who know their God will display strength and take action.*
> [33] *And those who have insight among the people will give understanding to the many...* (Daniel 11:32–33)

The prophecy continues,

> [3] *And those who have insight will shine brightly like the brightness of the expanse of heaven, and those who lead the many to righteousness, like the stars forever and ever.* (Daniel 12:3)

The River of Life

According to Daniel's prophecy, in the midst of great deception there will be a time and a people who know their God, have great insight, do exploits, and lead many to righteousness. They will receive a new and powerful endorsement of God's Spirit.

Additionally, if we know that the enemy will be warring specifically against the Holy Covenant, we can assume that insight into Christ's covenant will be a major weapon the saints will be able to use against Satan! With this in mind, in a fresh way the Holy Spirit is unveiling Christ's willingness to covenant with the Father for man's redemption.

As we are conformed to the nature and mission of Christ, a new authority is coming to Jesus' disciples, bringing with it redemptive power for our times and needs. And, while a great harvest is indeed prophesied for the end of this age, those leading the way will be individuals who understand Christ's covenant and have themselves covenanted with God for their land.

God's Unalterable Commitment

It is right to pray for the Lord to bless our lives. However, praying for the blessing and provision of God is not the same as covenanting with Him. A covenant is an altar upon which the Lord and His covenant partner give themselves fully to each other. The commitment we embrace is more compelling, more toward one another and less toward the needs of man. The quality of a covenant relationship with God does not cease once prayers have been answered, because in covenant love we mature from simply being believers to becoming living sacrifices, given to God's highest plans (Romans 12:1–2). By so yielding, He creates within us a life that He can use extraordinarily in the process of divine redemption.

Covenant power is greater than that which comes through prayer alone. The effects of a covenant reach far beyond simple faith. Prayer and faith are essentials: they are prerequisites, but not substitutes, for covenant power.

Thus, the covenant relationship is a lifelong pledge, an unbreakable oath that God Himself initiates and promises to sustain. Contained within His promise is His unalterable commitment, not only to satisfy His redemptive purposes, but to supply grace and faith to His human counterpart. Together, the All-Sufficient God and a believing person accomplish the impossible through their covenant relationship.

The Power Released in a Covenant

A covenant with God accomplishes two interconnected goals. It thrusts us beyond "subjective prayer" (prayer made primarily for our personal needs), and it brings us into a deeper commitment to God. Out of greater commitment comes greater grace to accomplish God's redemptive work in the world.

An example of covenant power is seen in ancient Israel during the revival that occurred after Athaliah, an idolatrous Judean queen, was dethroned. Jehoiada, the high priest, looked to God in covenant prayer. We read,

> ¹⁷ *Then Jehoiada made a covenant between the LORD and the king and the people, that they should be the LORD'S people, also between the king and the people.* (2 Kings 11:17)

The result of his covenant was that grace came upon the people and they cleansed the land of idolatry. We read, *"So all the people of the land rejoiced and the city was quiet"* (v. 20). Jehoiada's covenant brought the nation back to God and ended violence in Jerusalem!

Consider also the power released in Hezekiah's covenant with God. The nation of Judah had been fully corrupted by Ahaz, the preceding king. However, Hezekiah began his reign by seeking God's highest favor. He opened the doors of the temple and reconsecrated the priests.

Yet, the purification of priests and buildings by themselves would not have brought about revival had not Hezekiah taken one further step. He said,

¹⁰ *Now it is in my heart to make a covenant with the LORD God of Israel, that His burning anger may turn away from us.* (2 Chronicles 29:10)

Just eight days after the king made a covenant with the Lord, we read,

³⁶ *Then Hezekiah and all the people rejoiced over what God had prepared for the people, because the thing came about suddenly.* (2 Chronicles 29:36)

The difference between a long-term struggle and a speedy turning of the nation was, I believe, in the power that was released when the king covenanted with the Almighty.

It is vital that we, as Americans, remember that our spiritual forefathers were a people who knew and exercised principles of covenant sacrifice. When they came to this country, they knelt on its shores and covenanted with God for this land, dedicating this new world to Christ and His kingdom. It is unlikely that the revival of our nation will come about without local and national church leaders covenanting together with God for their land.

A Covenant with God

A personal covenant with God is a serious commitment, worthy of extended prayer and waiting before God. As He led, I personally have covenanted with Him to see the body of Christ delivered of carnal divisions and racism, that Christ's prayer in John 17 might be answered.

I have also united my life and faith with the covenants of our Pilgrim forefathers. Together with other brethren, both locally and nationally, we have covenanted with God to see this land restored, according to His covenantal promise, which is found in 2 Chronicles:

[14] *[If] My people who are called by My name humble themselves and pray, and seek My face and turn from their wicked ways, then I will hear from heaven, will forgive their sin, and will heal their land.* (2 Chronicles 7:14)

There will be a time when this nation, like all nations, becomes *"the kingdom of our Lord and of His Christ"* (Revelation 11:15). Until then, whether revival comes quickly or we pass through the fires of divine judgments, our lives belong to Christ —not simply to be blessed or prosperous, but to see His highest purposes accomplished in our land.

However, not all of us will covenant with God for the nation. According to their faith, some will make covenants with Him for their families. Others will covenant with God to see abortion ended in their cities. Still others will covenant with God for the church—to see the Lord's house built in their cities.

Making a covenant with God takes us further into our goal of Christlikeness. It is the highest relationship we can enjoy with God; it is that which brings Him the most pleasure. To those who covenant with God, He says,

> [5] *Gather My godly ones to Me, those who have made a covenant with Me by sacrifice.*   (Psalm 50:5)

Those Who Make a Covenant with God

Lord, open our hearts to the joy and wonder, the sobriety and fear of a covenant relationship with You. Lead us, O King, out of the superficial and into the supernatural. Lead us into a covenant with You for our nation! Amen.

10

"Ask of Me!"

We live in unparalleled times. Not since the first century have more Scriptures been fulfilled in a single generation. Each unfolding word brings down another mountain and lifts another valley. In truth, the way is being prepared for our King's return into this world.

The Great Revolt

The Lord forewarned that, during the end-times, *"many will go back and forth, and knowledge will increase"* (Daniel 12:4). Contrast our time with any other in history. Not only are we traveling farther and more frequently, but we do so in a world inundated with increasing knowledge. It has been our privilege to behold the prophetic return of Israel to its land (Jeremiah 16:14–15), and our misfortune to live when *"the earth is also polluted by its inhabitants..."* (Isaiah 24:5).

As though Jesus were reading a news summary of recent years, His prophecies of two thousand years ago clearly describe our times. He warned,

> [6] *And you will be hearing of wars and rumors of wars; see that you are not frightened, for those things must take place, but that is not yet the end.*
> [7] *For nation will rise against nation, and kingdom against kingdom, and in various places there will be famines and earthquakes.*

¹¹ *And many false prophets will arise,
and will mislead many.*
¹² *And because lawlessness is increased, most people's love will grow
cold.* (Matthew 24:6–7, 11–12)

These prophecies, among others, compel us to discern accurately the significant
times in which we live. Of all the prophetic
words being fulfilled in our day, one prophecy in particular arises with immediate im-
plications. It concerns the apostasy. Paul
warned, *"Let no one in any way deceive
you, for* [the day of the Lord] *will not come
unless the apostasy comes first"* (2 Thessalonians 2:3).

The apostasy has traditionally been
perceived as a time when many leave the
faith, a great *"falling away"* (2 Thessalonians 2:3 KJV) that precedes the coming of
the Antichrist. Depending upon your spe-
cific viewpoint, somewhere surrounding
these events is the rapture and the Lord's
return. However, the concept of apostasy
merely as a *"falling away"* is incomplete.
The original Greek word for apostasy,
apostasia, when it was used in classical

Greek literature, meant "a political revolt." From this we understand that the end-time apostasy is not just a time of expanded moral compromise; it is a time of open defiance and warlike aggression, a political insurrection, against the laws of God.

This interpretation of the apostasy is not an isolated view. The NIV, RSV, Today's English Version, Phillip's Translation and the New English Bible all render *apostasia* as *"the rebellion."* The Living Bible interprets the term as the *"great rebellion,"* while the Jerusalem Bible assigns a proper name, *"The Great Revolt."*

As we gaze in awe at the fulfillment of so many prophecies, let us carefully observe that mankind has entered an era of open revolt and outright rebellion, an apostasy, against the moral standards of God.

From God's Standards to No Standards

Today, we are witnessing a large-scale rebellion against godliness and moral values. This brazen attitude has had a name for itself since the 1960s—the sexual revolution—and revolution is exactly what it is. Our traditional moral standards have not only been challenged, but have been replaced by a non-standard, one that seeks to tolerate, and even promote, every sin from obscenity to homosexuality and witchcraft!

Those caught up in this mutiny against morality boldly defy the sway of God in our nation. They argue the only standard Americans have is the standard of individual freedom. In their view, freedom itself is the "god" ruling America, while the predominant religion is not Christianity, but rather self-indulgence.

However, those who wrote our constitution developed their sense of values during The Great Awakening, which began in 1735. This period of revival was possibly the most remarkable Christian era in American history. Our ancestors were born into a society almost entirely protected by Judeo-Christian ethics. It was this foundation of biblical standards that gave our freedom its virtue. Without it, liberty would have degenerated into lawlessness.

America in the Balance

To win the election, Bill Clinton has made political alliances with those spearheading the Great Revolt. Owning the "rights" to his promises, they will constantly pressure him toward ungodliness.

For this reason, we must pray all the more fervently for President Clinton. Let us also ask God to sever the pledges Clinton made with those in rebellion and forgive us and our President. In our prayers we must remember that Bill Clinton has made a number of public confessions of faith in Jesus Christ. Clinton is not our enemy; he is an imperfect man for whom Jesus died. If ever a man needed our prayers, it is our President. Our confidence is this: the same eternal Voice that convicted us concerning our sins is fully capable of reaching Bill Clinton. Our primary and most powerful access to him is not through lobbying or protesting, but praying to God.

Many of us have felt deep sorrow and even outrage over Clinton's pro-abortion position and his apparent eagerness to mainstream homosexuality. To all who *"sigh and groan"* (Ezekiel 9:4) over the abominations committed in America, remember that Jesus Christ remains Lord! According to God's word, *"He will faithfully bring forth justice. He will not be disheartened or crushed, until He has established justice in the earth"* (Isaiah 42:3–4). If Christ is not disheartened or crushed, let us also be unwavering.

Still, for those who prayed that America would vote against pro-abortion candidates, many questions remain unanswered. Not the least of these is, What does the outcome of our elections signify? Many believers are confused amidst the frenzy of Christian articles warning of Clinton and his policies. Let me also direct a warning, not concerning the President, but to those who have made him their enemy: *"Our struggle is not against flesh and blood"* (Ephesians 6:12). The moment we direct our anger toward a man, we forfeit the influence of God (James 1:20).

Since we believe God answers prayer, then we must conclude that Bill Clinton's election is connected to a larger, more encompassing, strategy from God. Christ is after more than a seat on the Republican platform. For those of us in the right wing, we must pray for the redemption of the left wing, asking God to rescue the sincerely deceived of this nation.

"And the two wings of the great eagle were given to the woman..." (Revelation 12:14). Whether this verse refers to America or not, my faith tells me God is willing to give both the conservative and liberal "wings" of our nation to the "woman," the church. Those Christians who soar on the right-wing issues—morality and pro-life— need to appreciate such left-wing concerns as helping the poor, healing racial issues, and protecting the earth. These mandates are equally biblical.

Because the rebellion has been sheltered under the left wing, we have been guilty of overreacting and condemning this entire side of our national conscience. Likewise, the left wing can point to the right-wing extremes of the KKK and bigotry. They can easily include us in their denunciation. The outcome of all of our finger-pointing is that we fail to hear the heart of those from both sides who make the eagle fly.

Jesus wants all of this nation. Unfortunately, the focus of our prayers has been more crisis-oriented than Christ-oriented. Thus, to reach America, God is purifying the heart of the prayer movement until we reflect all of His desires.

Did we want to win the election so we could return to a passive prayer life? Were we looking more for the sigh of relief than God's view of a larger harvest? Jesus always lives to make intercession for us (Hebrews 7:25). Not until we also live to pray will the maturity of the prayer movement be complete.

You see, as part of God's bigger plan, He is calling us to become like Jesus. We must learn to bless those who curse us and to pray for those who persecute us (Luke 6:28). He is making "sons" out of us. Thus, national elections may not have purified our government, but they should have a purifying effect upon the church, provided we become Christlike in our intercession. In a greater way, we will be forced to become true New Testament Christians!

The apostasy will certainly intensify, but we must remember it is only one of many prophecies unfolding in our day. The same Divine Word that warned of the rebellion also purposed that His kingdom will crush and put an end to all nations (Daniel 2:44). For Christians, our most serious loss is not political but spiritual—the loss of our vision of God's kingdom.

Therefore, the greatest political strategy we can employ is to walk as mature citizens of God's kingdom (Philippians 3:20). Yes, evil will mature into full rebellion, but good is also ripening into full Christlikeness! (See Matthew 13:40–43; John 17:22–23.) Yes, the apostasy will reveal the nature of Satan, but the true church will manifest the glory of God! Jesus is not only coming in the skies, but also He is coming *"to be glorified in His saints on that day, and to be marveled at among all who have believed"* (2 Thessalonians 1:10). What seems to be Satan's hour now, full of darkness and rebellion, is simply the opportunity for grace to abound to the glory of God in the church!

Seated with Christ!

The second Psalm, perhaps more then any other text, accurately portrays the spirit of our times and our correct response to it. Although it was quoted by the early church (Acts 4:25–26), God has set its full realization for the end of this age.

> [1] *Why are the nations in an uproar, and the peoples devising a vain thing?*
> [2] *The kings of the earth take their stand, and the rulers take counsel together against the LORD and against His Anointed:*
> [3] *Let us tear their fetters apart, and cast away their cords from us!*
>
> (Psalm 2:1–3)

Although the rebellion reveals itself worldwide in many ways, in America many of our leaders have most certainly been counseling together *"against the LORD"* in their recent decisions. We see it in the legal protection offered to the gay movement and the shelter provided for satanic rock music. Again, our anti-censorship laws, like armor plating, take their stand against the Lord as they shield our sick entertainment industry. Through almost every media form, the cry of those in rebellion hammers relentlessly upon the fetters of moral restraint, all with government backing!

This railing against God is not going unnoticed in heaven. Yet, is the Almighty confounded? Has fear concerning recent developments gripped the Lord's heart? No. The Psalm continues,

> [4] *He who sits in the heavens laughs.*
> *The Lord scoffs at them.*
> [5] *Then He will speak to them in His*
> *anger and terrify them in His fury.*
> (Psalm 2:4–5)

The Lord laughs at the foolishness of those in the rebellion when they imagine God's judgments cannot reach them. In truth, our cities' decline, the AIDS crisis, our insurmountable national debt, and the

breakdown of our families are all conse-
quences of our sins, the result of God's dis-
approval with our nation.

Can the Lord reach and redeem this
nation? Consider the Soviet communists.
For decades they shook their fists toward
God, proclaiming atheism as the national
religion. Their cosmonauts came back from
space missions mocking Christianity, as
they stated they saw no God in heaven.
Then the Lord arose. In His predetermined
time He simply looked at those who railed,
"There is no God." When He spoke, "There
is no communism," the structure of the Soviet Empire crumbled from the inside out.

Even as He undermined their rebellion
against Him and today Russia is experi-
encing a national spiritual awakening, so
the voice of God will once again come to
America. He will shake this nation and
gather to Himself a mighty harvest.

God Is Waiting for Us

Why, you ask, does the Lord delay His
full judgment? As the Lord waited for the

"iniquity of the Amorite" (Genesis 15:16) to become full prior to giving Canaan to Israel, so His justice demands that the rebellion should fill up the full measure of guilt before final judgments come.

Yet, more than waiting for evil to ripen, the Lord waits for us, His church. While the world will demand, and receive, the reign of hell, the goal of the praying church will be for the reign of heaven. You see, all of God's prophecies will be fulfilled—those concerning evil and those concerning good. The Lord has purposed to have a bride *"in all her glory, having no spot or wrinkle or any such thing; but that she should be holy and blameless"* (Ephesians 5:27), and a kingdom of wheat without tares (Matthew 13:24–30). The transformation of the church will be fulfilled as surely as the increase of knowledge, the return of Israel, and the apostasy itself.

Thus, with great fear and holy trembling, we must review what God has promised concerning us, His church! Let us remember that the Lord is not alone in the heavens. According to His Word, He has seated us with Him in the heavenly places (Ephesians 2:6). It is time for our identity as Christians to shift. We are Americans only by virtue of our ambassador status; our true citizenship is in heaven (Philippians 3:20). And if God is laughing at the mocking of those in the rebellion (Psalm 2:2, 4), let us also, as His subjects, share His confidence!

God has a day of reckoning against every proud and lofty nation. As communism has fallen, so the materialism and pride of this nation will also bow to our king. What will remain is His kingdom, which cannot be shaken (Hebrews 12:27–28)! God is moving us into the spirit of His kingship now, so that we may proclaim the *"gospel of the kingdom"* (Matthew 24:14) before Christ's return!

Thus, He tells us to sit with Him in the completeness of His purpose. He commands us not only to live without fear, but also to stand in prayer for these very nations that defy Him! Listen again to this second Psalm, for in the very context of

worldwide rebellion against Him, it records
the most remarkable discourse:

> [8] *Ask of Me,* [the Father says to the
> Son] *and I will surely give the nations
> as Thine inheritance, and the very
> ends of the earth as Thy possession.*
>
> (Psalm 2:8)

This request has little to do with the
goodness of the church, but everything to
do with the virtue of Christ and the love of
the Father toward Him. Look around you:
twenty years ago this nation was cold in its
prayer. Today leaders of denominations
comprising 180,000 churches in America
are calling their churches to unite in sup-
plication for this nation. Jesus has asked
the Father for America, and in response
the prayer movement has been born!

As Christ's church, we do not deserve a
national revival, but Jesus does! As His
representatives, in His name and virtue,
we ask of the Father for this nation! More
than an expression of faith, our prayer is
an act of obedience: we are ordered to ask
Him!

Therefore, while the perverse strive toward complete rejection of God, even as their mocking words fill the air with curses, God's unchangeable promise to us is this: *"Ask of Me, and I will surely give the nations!"*

While you sit in jail for your protest against abortion, even as witchcraft flourishes in our schools, while our government leaders counsel against the Lord—ASK!

Put away discouragement. Repent of fretting. The more we accept our place in the divine plan, the more we also shall learn to dwell with Christ in the heavens, where we laugh at the enemy. In spite of the world around us, we simply do what God commanded: ask Him for the nations!

The faith that relentlessly asks God also pleases God. Now, as the fullness of the times unfolds, as the world around us clothes itself in prophetic fufilllments, let us put away fear and repent of withdrawal, for it is a time to ask of God. He will give this nation as an inheritance to Christ!